FUN JOKES!

FOR FUNNY KIDS

Reader's
Digest

New York / Montreal

A Note from the Editors

Reader's Digest is the world's #1 collector of humor for everyone from age 6 to 106. In *Fun Jokes for Funny Kids, Volume 3*, we've compiled the best of the best for our youngest readers. We asked two clever sisters to tell us which ones they liked most—you'll see Alexa's Favorites and Arya's Favorites sprinkled throughout the book.

Now we're inviting parents of budding comedians to send jokes for our next volume. Submit your child's riddles, one-liners, puns, and more at **rd.com/jokesforkids**.

About Alexa and Arya

Alexa is a fourth grader who lives in New York City. She loves gymnastics, the color pink, and eating tacos and tuna.

Arya is Alexa's sister. She is in first grade and prefers purple. She also likes swimming and cats.

Table of Contents

Knock!
Knock!

Eggcited

Knock! Knock!
  Who's there?
Egg.
  Egg who?
Eggcited to see me?

Together We Go

Knock! Knock!
  Who's there.
Grub.
  Grub who?
Grub hold of my hand and let's go.

Quick!

Knock! Knock!
  Who's there?
Butter.
  Butter who?
Butter be quick, I have to go to the bathroom.

---------- ★ **ALEXA'S FAVORITE**

Justice

Knock! Knock!

Who's there?

Justice.

Justice who?

Justice once, let me in please.

- -

Second Place

Knock! Knock!

Who's there?

The guy who finished second.

The guy who finished second who?

Exactly.

Locked Out

Knock! Knock!

Who's there?

Mikey.

Mikey who?

Mi-key isn't working. Can you let me in?

Superman

Knock! Knock!
  Who's there?
Soup.
  Soup who?
Superman!

---------- ★ **ALEXA'S FAVORITE**

Come Closer

Knock! Knock!
  Who's there?
Lena.
  Lena who?
Lena little closer and I'll tell you.

Under Arrest

Knock! Knock!
  Who's there?
Hans.
  Hans who?
Hans up—you're under arrest!

You Know Me

Knock! Knock!
  Who's there?
Juno.
  Juno who?
Juno it's me, so let me in now!

Pigs Fly

Knock! Knock!
  Who's there?
Oink oink.
  Oink oink who?
Make up your mind—are you a pig or an owl?

Holiday Greeting

Knock! Knock!
  Who's there?
Mary and Abby.
  Mary and Abby who?
Mary Christmas and Abby New Year.

Stick Up!

Knock! Knock!
   Who's there?
Razor!
   Razor who?
Razor hands, this is a stickup!

This Seems Familiar

Knock! Knock!
   Who's there?
Dejav.
   Dejav who?
Knock! Knock!

Poet and You Don't Even Know It

Knock! Knock!
   Who's there?
Hike.
   Hike who?
I didn't know you liked Japanese poetry.

Mistaken Identity

Knock! Knock!
   Who's there?
I am.
   I am who?
You tell me!

- - - - - - - - - - ★ **ALEXA'S FAVORITE**

Break Down

Knock! Knock!
   Who's there?
Stan.
   Stan who?
Stan back 'cause I'm going to break down the door!

- -

Gladys Is at the Door

Knock! Knock!
   Who's there?
Gladys.
   Gladys who?
Gladys the weekend—no homework!

Off to the Store

Knock! Knock!
  Who's there?
Kiwi.
  Kiwi who?
Kiwi go to the store?

Who!

Knock! Knock!
  Who's there?
Cook.
  Cook who?
Hey! Who are you calling cuckoo?

- - - - - - - - - - ★ **ALEXA'S FAVORITE**

One More Time

Knock! Knock!
  Who's there?
Alaska.
  Alaska who?
Alaska just one more time.

- -

Locked Door

Knock! Knock!
  Who's there?
Theodore.
  Theodore who?
Theodore is locked, so please let me in!

Had to Meet You

Knock! Knock!
  Who's there?
Norma Lee.
  Norma Lee who?
Norma Lee I don't go around knocking on doors, but I just had to meet you.

School Today

Knock! Knock!
  Who's there?
Dewey.
  Dewey who?
Dewey have to go to school today?

Guitar

Knock! Knock!
   Who's there?
Guitar.
   Guitar who?
Guitar coats, it's cold outside.

Lion

Knock! Knock!
   Who's there?
Lion.
   Lion who?
Lion on your doorstep! Open up.

Bath Time

Knock! Knock!
   Who's there?
Dwayne.
   Dwayne who?
Dwayne the bathtub already. I'm dwowning.

Pinch

Knock! Knock!
   Who's there?
Pinch.
   Pinch who?
I'm gonna pinch you unless you open this door.

- -

Beehive

Knock! Knock!
   Who's there?
Beehive.
   Beehive who?
Beehive yourself or you'll get into trouble.

Missing You

Knock! Knock!
   Who's there?
Amish.
   Amish who?
Awe, I miss you too.

Stranger

Knock! Knock!
   Who's there?
Some.
   Some who?
Someday you'll recognize me, hopefully.

--------- ★ **ALEXA'S FAVORITE**

Doesn't Ring a Bell

Knock! Knock!
   Who's there?
Nobel.
   Nobel who?
No bell, that's why I knocked!

Pooh

Knock! Knock!
   Who's there?
Pooh.
   Pooh who?
Don't you know Winnie the Pooh?

Can't

Knock! Knock!
   Who's there?
Cantaloupe.
   Cantaloupe who?
You cantaloupe, you're too young to get married.

Not Leaving

Knock! Knock!
   Who's there?
Norway.
   Norway who?
Norway I am leaving, so open up.

Love

Knock! Knock!
   Who's there?
I love.
   I love who?
You forgot who you love?

Ridiculous
Riddles

2 to 1

Q: What makes two people out of one?

A: A mirror.

---------- ★ **ARYA'S FAVORITE**

Black and White

Q: What is white when it is dirty, and black when clean?

A: A blackboard.

A Fish with No Eye

Q: What do you call a fish with no eye?

A: Fsh.

Walls

Q: What ancient invention allows people to see through walls?

A: A window.

Dog Crossing

Q: A man stands on one side of a river, his dog on the other. The man calls his dog, who immediately crosses the river without getting wet and without using a bridge or a boat. How did the dog do it?

A: The river was frozen.

Take a Look

Q: What has lots of eyes but can't see?

A: A potato.

Full View

Q: There are 20 people in an empty, square room. Each person has full sight of the entire room and everyone in it without turning his head or body, or moving in any way (other than the eyes). Where can you place an apple so that all but one person can see it?

A: Place the apple on one person's head.

Math Time

Q: How can the number four be half of five?

A: IV, the Roman numeral for four, which is "half" (two letters) of the word five "V."

Sharpen Up

Q: What gets sharper the more you use it?

A: Your brain.

Lummox

Q: Turn us on our backs and open up our stomachs, and you will be the wisest but at the start a lummox. What are we?

A: Books.

Dinner

Q: You bought me for dinner but never eat me. What am I?

A: Cutlery.

---------- ★ ARYA'S FAVORITE

Cruising Along

Q: You see a boat filled with people. It has not sunk, but when you look again, you don't see a single person on the boat. Why?

A: All the people were married.

Easy Peasy

Q: Which word in the dictionary is always spelled incorrectly?

A: Incorrectly.

Water Kills

Q: I am not alive, but I grow; I don't have lungs but I need air; water kills me. What am I?

A: Fire.

---------- ★ **ARYA'S FAVORITE**

Hard As a Rock

Q: What is hard as rock, but melts immediately in hot water?

A: Ice cubes.

Weight for It

Q: Which is heavier: a ton of bricks or a ton of feathers?

A: Neither, they both weigh the same.

In Love

Q: A doctor and a bus driver are both in love with the same woman, an attractive girl named Sarah. The bus driver had to go on a long bus trip that would last a week. Before he left, he gave Sarah seven apples. Why?

A: An apple a day keeps the doctor away!

Six Faces

Q: What has six faces, but doesn't wear makeup. Twenty-one eyes, but cannot see?

A: A die (dice).

Cluck Life

Q: Why does a chicken coop have two doors?

A: If it had four, it would be a chicken sedan.

Impossible to Say 'Yes'

Q: What answer can you never answer yes to?

A: Are you asleep yet?

Holds Water

Q: What is full of holes but still holds water?

A: A sponge.

Not What You Think

Q: First, think of the color of the clouds. Next, think of the color of snow. Now, think of the color of a bright full moon. Now answer quickly: What do cows drink?

A: Water.

Black/Red/Gray

Q: What is black when you buy it, red when you use it, and gray when you throw it away?

A: Charcoal.

Time

Q: You have me today; tomorrow you'll have more. as your time passes, I'm not easy to store. I don't take up space, but I'm only in one place. I am what you saw, but not what you see. What am I?

A: Memories.

More

Q: The more you take, the more you leave behind—what are they?

A: Footprints.

Four Wheels

Q: What has four wheels and flies?

A: A garbage truck.

---------- ★ **ARYA'S FAVORITE**

Just Up Ahead

Q: I am always in front of you and never behind you. What am I?

A: Your future.

Talk the Talk

Q: What can you hear, but not see or touch, even though you control it?

A: Your voice.

Take a Seat

Q: What has legs, but doesn't walk?

A: A table.

Bless You!

Q: What can you catch, but not throw?

A: A cold.

Every Direction

Q: What can point in every direction but can't reach the destination by itself?

A: Your finger.

- - - - - - - - - ★ ARYA'S FAVORITE

Sunnyside Up

Q: I have to be opened, but I don't have a lid or a key to get in. What am I?

A: An egg.

- -

Everyone's Need

Q: Almost everyone needs it, asks for it, gives it, but almost never takes it. What is it?

A: Advice.

What Am I???

Q: I have keys but no doors; I have space but no rooms; I allow you to enter but you are never able to leave. What am I?

A: A keyboard.

Rock On

Q: What kind of band never plays music?

A: A rubber band.

Buried?

Q: Why can't someone living in Maine be buried in Florida?

A: Because he's still living!

No Sleep

Q: How can a man go eight days without sleep?

A: He only sleeps at night.

Monkey Business

Q: There are two monkeys on a tree and one jumps off. Why does the other monkey jump too?

A: Monkey see, monkey do!

T Time

Q: What begins with T, finishes with T, and has T in it?

A: A teapot.

Watch Out

Q: What has hands, but can't clap?

A: A clock.

Daddy Issues

Q: How can you physically stand behind your father while he is standing behind you?

A: You are standing back-to-back with your father.

---------- ★ ARYA'S FAVORITE

Nighttime

Q: What comes out at night without being called, and is lost in the day without being stolen?

A: Stars.

Inside Out

Q: First, I threw away the outside and cooked the inside. Then I ate the outside and threw away the inside. What did I eat?

A: Corn on the cob.

The Last Place

Q: When you look for something, why is it always in the last place you look?

A: Because when you find it, you stop looking.

---------- ★ ARYA'S FAVORITE

The Long Line

Q: You draw a line. Without touching it, how do you make it a longer line?

A: Draw a short line next to it and now it's the longer line.

Play Outside

Q: I run along your property and all around the backyard, yet I never move. What am I?

A: A fence.

Family Numbers

Q: Your parents have six sons including you and each son has one sister. How many people are in the family?

A: Nine—two parents, six sons, and one daughter.

Cutting and Grinding

Q: I'm white, and used for cutting and grinding. When I'm damaged, humans usually remove me or fill me. For most animals I am a useful tool.

A: A tooth!

Giveaway

Q: You cannot keep me until you have given me. What am I?

A: Your word.

Word Play

Q: What word in the English language does the following: the first two letters signify a male, the first three letters signify a female, the first four letters signify greatness, while the entire word signifies a great woman. What is the word?

A: Heroine.

A Handy Question

Q: What has four fingers and a thumb, but isn't alive?

A: A glove.

In, On and Around

Q: What do you always have in you and sometimes on you; and if I surround you, I could kill you?

A: Water.

---------- ★ **ARYA'S FAVORITE**

Sweet Treat

Q: What kind of cup doesn't hold water?

A: A cupcake.

Best Pals

Q: I am often following you and copying your every move. Yet you can never touch me or catch me. What am I?

A: A shadow.

Line Up

Q: What are the next three letters in this combination? OTTFFSS

A: E N T (Each letter represents the first letter in the written numbers: One, Two, Three, Four, Five, etc.).

Quirky
Q & A's

Beach Bank

Q: Why did the banker open a bank at the beach?

A: To hold sand dollars!

- - - - - - - - - ★ **ALEXA'S FAVORITE**

Count on Us

Q: When things go wrong, what can you always count on?

A: Your fingers.

- -

The Perfect Fit

Q: How long does it take to know if a pair of underwear fits you well?

A: Just a brief moment!

Which State?

Q: Which Southern state is most stood on?

A: Floor-ida.

Play It By Ear

Q: Why did the pianist keep banging his head against the keys?

A: He was playing by ear.

I'll Take Mine to Go

Q: Why go to the paint store when you're on a diet?

A: You can get thinner there.

A Question of Time

Q: I'm the rare case when today comes before yesterday. What am I?

A: A dictionary.

Bad for Your Teeth

Q: What's red and bad for your teeth?

A: A brick.

Butter

Q: Why did the boy throw butter out the window?

A: He wanted to see the butterfly.

Cold Feet

Q: Why was the dead man not courageous?

A: Because he had cold feet.

Buy a Vowel

Q: You see me once in June, twice in November, but not at all in May. What am I?

A: The letter "e".

For Young Padawans

Q: What do you call a droid that likes taking the scenic route?

A: R2-Detour!

Generation Gap

Q: What do you call it when you have your mom's mom on speed dial?

A: Insta-gram.

Computer Commute

Q: Why did the computer show up at work late?

A: It had a hard drive.

- - - - - - - - - - ★ ALEXA'S FAVORITE

Curious Letter

Q: Which is the most curious letter?

A: Y

- -

He Gets Life

Q: Why was the dead man happy to be sentenced during his trial?

A: Because they gave him life.

A's

Q: Why are A's like flowers?

A: Because bees come after them!

Dead Lawyer

Q: How come nobody liked the dead lawyer?

A: Because he was rotten to the core.

---------- ★ **ALEXA'S FAVORITE**

Pirate Payment

Q: How much did the pirate pay for his peg and hook?

A: An arm and a leg.

- -

Forrest Gump

Q: What's Forrest Gump's password?

A: 1Forrest1.

Amish Guy...

Q: What do you call an Amish guy with his hand in a horse's mouth?

A: A mechanic.

Sea Creature

Q: What do you call a monster with no neck?

A: The Lost Neck Monster.

Accidental Murder

Q: What did the axe murderer say to the judge?

A: It was an axe-ident.

What Are Two Things...

Q: What are two things you wouldn't eat after waking up?

A: Lunch and dinner.

Signal Change

Q: Why does a traffic light turn red?

A: You would too if you had to change in front of so many people.

Stage Fright

Q: Did you hear about the actor who fell through the floorboards?

A: He was just going through a stage.

On Shore

Q: Why don't pirates take a shower before they walk the plank?

A: They just wash up on shore.

Dots and Dashes

Q: What do you call an apology written in dots and dashes?

A: Re-Morse code.

--------- ★ **ALEXA'S FAVORITE**

Superman's Costume

Q: Why are all of Superman's costumes tight?

A: They're all size S.

Average

Q: Where are average things manufactured?

A: The satisfactory.

Bubblegum Ride

Q: What do you call a train carrying bubblegum?

A: A chew-chew train.

Literally Speaking

Q: How many letters are in the alphabet?

A: There are 11 letters in "the alphabet."

Cold Artists

Q: Why do artists constantly feel cold?

A: Because they're surrounded by drafts.

Vowels

Q: Is there one word that contains all the vowels?

A: Unquestionably.

---------- ★ ALEXA'S FAVORITE

Lifeguard

Q: What's a lifeguard's favorite game?

A: Pool.

Can Opener

Q: What do you call a can opener that doesn't work?

A: A can't opener!

Batman

Q: Where does Batman go to the bathroom?

A: The batroom.

Subtraction

Q: How many times can you subtract 10 from 100?

A: Once. The next time, you would be subtracting 10 from 90.

Air Walk

Q: How do you walk without touching the ground?

A: Walk on an airplane!

Parlé

Q: What did one Frenchman say to the other?

A: I have no idea; I don't speak French.

Timepiece

Q: A sundial has the fewest moving parts of any timepiece. Which has the most?

A: An hourglass—It has thousands of grains of sand.

Running

Q: What's the difference between a man and a dog running?

A: One wears trousers and the other pants.

Sick Pig

Q: What do you give a sick pig?

A: Oink-ment!

No Surfing

Q: What wave can't you surf on?

A: A micro-wave!

Tissue Dance

Q: How do you make a tissue dance?

A: Put a little boogie in it.

---------- ★ **ALEXA'S FAVORITE**

I Quit

Q: Why did the can-crusher quit his job?

A: Because it was soda-pressing.

Big, Bigger, Biggest

Q: Who is bigger: Mr. Bigger or Mr. Bigger's baby?

A: The baby is a little Bigger.

Smelly Ship

Q: Do you know what stinks about a pirate ship?

A: The poop deck.

---------- ★ **ALEXA'S FAVORITE**

Frying Pan

Q: Why is Europe like a frying pan?

A: Because it has Greece at the bottom.

Bored Surfer

Q: What do you call a surfer when he has nothing to do?

A: Surf bored!

One Leg

Q: What do you call a woman with one leg?

A: Eileen.

Lightning Dates

Q: Where do lightning bolts go on dates?

A: To Cloud 9.

Balloon Music

Q: What kind of music are balloons afraid of?

A: Pop music.

Seattle Rain

Q: What do you call two straight days of rain in Seattle?

A: A weekend.

The Angry Pirate

Q: How do you make a pirate furious?

A: Take away the p.

Precisely!

Q: What's the difference between ignorance and apathy?

A: I don't know and I don't care.

Medical Q&A's

Did You Hear...

Q: Did you hear the one about the germ?

A: Never mind, I don't want to spread it around.

Doctor Annoyed

Q: When is a doctor most annoyed?

A: When he is out of patients.

Red Pen

Q: Why did the nurse need a red pen at work?

A: In case she needed to draw blood.

Ring, Ring

Q: Doctor, I keep hearing a ringing sound.

A: Then answer the phone!

54

---------- ★ **ALEXA'S FAVORITE**

Apple a Day

Q: Does an apple a day keep the doctor away?

A: Only if you aim it well enough.

- -

Queen's Teeth

Q: Why did the queen go to the dentist?

A: To get her teeth crowned!

Skeleton Visit

Q: Why did the skeleton go to the doctor?

A: Because he wouldn't stop coffin!

Lips Sealed

Q: Why didn't the girl tell the doctor that she ate some glue?

A: Her lips were sealed.

Shaking Cabinet

Q: Why did the man shake the medicine cabinet?

A: To wake up the sleeping pills!

---------- ★ **ALEXA'S FAVORITE**

Window Doctor

Q: What did the doctor say to the window?

A: Have any new panes (pains)?

Pen and Pencil

Patient: Doctor, Doctor, come quickly. My son just swallowed a pen!

Doctor: Use a pencil till I get there!

Humpty Dumpty

Q: Why did Humpty Dumpty go to a psychiatrist?

A: He was cracking up!

Shake Well

Q: Why does your sister jump up and down before taking her medicine?

A: Because the label says "Shake well before using!"

Blood Test

Q: What do you get when you mix a vampire and a doctor?

A: A blood test!

Invisible

Patient: Doctor, sometimes I feel like I'm invisible.

Doctor: Who said that?

Beekeeper

Q: Why did the beekeeper go to the doctor?

A: She had hives!

Please Don't Administer Orally

Mother: My son must have a temperature. He hasn't taken our motorcycle out all day.

Doctor: Do you have a thermometer?

Mother: No, a Kawasaki.

Double Vision

Patient: Doctor, Doctor, I keep seeing double!

Doctor: Sit on the couch.

Patient: Which one?

How Am I?

Q: Did you hear about the two psychiatrists who passed each other on a walk?

A: One said to the other, "You're fine, How am I?"

Need Glasses?

Q: Doctor, I need glasses!

A: Yeah, you do, cause you're in the pizza parlor!

Rocket Ship

Q: **What did the doctor say to the rocket ship?**

A: Time to get your booster shot.

---------- ★ **ALEXA'S FAVORITE**

Tonsils

Q: **What did one tonsil say to the other tonsil?**

A: Let's dress up! The doctor is taking us out!

One-Liners

Spaghetti Bike

● ● ●

I told my mom I was going to make a bike out of spaghetti. You should have seen her face when I rode straight pasta.

Air and Space

● ● ●

I visited the Air and Space Museum... Nothing was there.

Too Much Time

● ● ●

I ate a clock yesterday. It was very time-consuming.

Lean Forward

● ● ●

Sometimes I tuck my knees into my chest and lean forward. That's just how I roll.

Average People
• • •

Average people are so mean!

When a Grizzly Means Business
• • •

Stand back, or I'll beat you with
my bear hands!

---------- ★ ARYA'S FAVORITE

Boiling Water
• • •

Rest in peace to boiling water.
You will be mist.

Greasy Love
• • •

Don't go bacon my heart.
I couldn't if I fried.

Tomato Love

• • •

I love you from my head tomatoes.

Message from the Dog

• • •

Once my dog ate all the Scrabble tiles.
For days he kept leaving little messages
around the house.

---------- ★ ARYA'S FAVORITE

Light Reading

• • •

I was reading a book on helium.
I couldn't put it down.

Rock, Paper, Ticket

• • •

Do I lose when the police officer says
papers and I say scissors?

Peanut Stroll

• • •

Two peanuts were walking down the street.
One was a salted!

Lacking Courage

• • •

I wanted to tell a skeleton pun, but I don't
have the guts for it.

Hurdle

• • •

I used to have a fear of hurdles,
but I got over it.

A Dumb Driver's-Ed Answer

• • •

My sister didn't do as well on her
driver's-ed test as she'd hoped. It might
have had something to do with how she
completed this sentence: "When the _____
is dead, the car won't start."
She wrote: "Driver."

Wacky
Animals

Dinosaur Car Crash

Q: What do you get when two dinosaurs crash their cars?

A: T-Rex.

---------- ★ ALEXA'S FAVORITE

Lazy Kangaroo

Q: What do you call a lazy kangaroo?

A: A pouch potato.

Who Pays the Bill?

Q: A rabbit and a duck went to dinner. Who paid?

A: The duck—he had the bill.

Door Frog

Q: What job did the frog have at the hotel?

A: Bellhop.

Charging Bull

Q: What's the first thing you should do if a bull charges you?

A: Pay him!

Exploding

Q: What do you call an ape that is exploding?

A: A baboom!

Spoiled Kitty

Q: What do you call a cat that gets anything it wants?

A: Purr-suasive.

Magician Owl

Q: What do you call an owl that does magic tricks?

A: Hoodini.

Thief!

Q: What do you call a thieving alligator?

A: A crookodile.

Koalas

Q: Why aren't koalas actual bears?

A: They don't meet the koalafications.

Pig Secret

Q: Why should you never trust a pig with a secret?

A: Because he's bound to squeal.

Shark Diet

Q: What did the shark say when he ate the clownfish?

A: This tastes a little funny.

Fancy Fish

Q: What do you call a classy fish?

A: Sofishticated.

No Eyes

Q: What do you call a deer with no eyes?

A: No-eye-deer.

Water Ants

Q: Why can't male ants sink?

A: They're buoy-ant.

---------- ★ ALEXA'S FAVORITE

Skunk Trial

Q: What did the judge say when the skunk came into his courtroom?

A: "Odor in the court!"

- -

Sleeping Bull

Q: **What do you call a bull when he is sleeping?**

A: A bulldozer.

Hide-and-Seek

Q: **Why is it so hard for a leopard to hide?**

A: Because he's always spotted.

Toothless Bear

Q: **What do you call a bear with no teeth?**

A: A gummy bear.

- - - - - - - - - - ★ **ALEXA'S FAVORITE**

Prehistoric Humor

Q: **Why did the dinosaur cross the road?**

A: Because chickens didn't exist yet!

- -

Flea-ing the Scene

Q: What type of market should you NEVER take your dog to?

A: A flea market!

Over-Caffeinated Kangaroo

Q: Why did the kangaroo stop drinking coffee?

A: She got too jumpy!

Car Animal

Q: What do you call an animal you keep in your car?

A: A carpet.

Sick Pony

Q: What do you call a pony with a cough?

A: A little horse.

Rise and Shine

Q: What time does a duck wake up?

A: At the quack of dawn!

Too Poor

Q: What did the cat say when he lost all his money?

A: I'm paw!

Trance

Q: What is big, muddy and sends people into a trance?

A: A hypno-potamus.

What Do Pandas Have...

Q: What do pandas have that no other animal has?

A: Baby pandas!

Shark Fun

Q: What is a shark's favorite game?

A: Swallow the leader!

---------- ★ ALEXA'S FAVORITE

Tiger Snack

Q: What do you call a tiger that ate your father's sister?

A: An aunt-eater!

Legless

Q: What do you call a lamb with no legs?

A: A cloud.

Silly Octopus

Q: How do you make an octopus laugh?

A: With ten-tickles.

Mix with Vinegar

Q: What do you get if you cross a cat with a bottle of vinegar?

A: A sourpuss.

Beware the Weather

Q: What happens when it rains cats and dogs?

A: I don't know but don't step in a poodle.

- - - - - - - - - - ★ **ALEXA'S FAVORITE**

Pterodactyl

Q: Why can't you hear a pterodactyl go to the bathroom?

A: Because the "P" is silent.

- -

Docked Mice

Q: Where do mice park their boats?

A: At hickory dickory dock.

Dry Penguin

Q: What do you call a penguin in the desert?

A: Lost.

Careful Where You Sit

Q: What did the dog say when he sat on sandpaper?

A: Ruff!

Green Jumper

Q: What is green and can jump a mile in a minute?

A: A grasshopper with hiccups!

Hardest Key

Q: What is the hardest key to turn?

A: A donkey.

Nine Lives

Q: What animal has more lives than a cat?

A: A toad—it's always croaking!

Wrinkled Elephants

Q: Why are elephants so wrinkled?

A: Because they take too long to iron.

Dangerous Selfie

Q: What do you call taking a selfie with a rattlesnake?

A: A misss-take.

Walrus

Q: What do you call a walrus in a phone booth?

A: Stuck.

Stack of Cats

Q: What do you call a big pile of cats?

A: A purramid.

- - - - - - - - - ★ ALEXA'S FAVORITE

Clumsy Fish

Q: What did the fish say when it swam into a wall?

A: "Dam!"

- -

Armed Alligator

Q: How many arms does an alligator have?

A: Depends on how far he is done with his dinner!

Game Day

Q: What is a turtle's favorite game?

A: Peekaboo.

Fish Bait

Q: How do you catch a school of fish?

A: With a bookworm.

Alligator

Q: What do you call an alligator in a vest?

A: An investigator!

Dog Chase

Q: Why did the dog chase his own tail?

A: He was trying to make both ends meet!

- - - - - - - - - - ★ **ALEXA'S FAVORITE**

Clever Animal?

Q: Which animal do you think is clever —
a cat or a dog?

A: A cat, of course. Have you ever seen a cat
pulling a sled through snow and ice?

Cross a Parrot...

Q: What do you get when you cross a parrot and a centipede?

A: A walkie-talkie.

Turtle/Giraffe

Q: What do you get if you cross a turtle with a giraffe?

A: A turtle-neck.

Séance

Q: Why did the chicken go to the séance?

A: To get to the other side.

Cross a Snake...

Q: If you cross a snake with a robin, what kind of bird would you get?

A: A swallow!

Crabs

Q: Why don't crabs give to charity?

A: Because they're shellfish.

Chocolate-Covered

Q: What do you call a lamb covered in chocolate?

A: A candy baaar.

Dinosaur Respect

Q: What do you call a dinosaur as tall as a house, with long, sharp teeth and 12 claws on each foot?

A: Sir.

Weight-Watchers

Q: What animals are weight-watchers?

A: Fish. They carry their scales with them at all times.

Crocodile GPS

Q: What do you call a crocodile with GPS?

A: A navigator.

---------- ★ ALEXA'S FAVORITE

Sorry Giraffes

Q: Why are giraffes so slow to apologize?

A: It takes them a long time to swallow their pride.

Cow Blast

Q: What would happen if a dairy cow exploded?

A: Udder madness!

Serpents Plus Sweets

Q: What do you get when you cross a snake with a tasty dessert?

A: A pie-thon!

Banking Frog

Q: Why did the frog wear a mask to the bank?

A: He said he wanted to "rob-bit."

- - - - - - - - - ★ ALEXA'S FAVORITE

Bad Storytellers

Q: Why are cats bad storytellers?

A: Because they only have one tale.

- -

Changing Spots

Q: How can a leopard change its spots?

A: By moving from one spot to another!

Three Ducks in a Box

Q: What do you get when you put three ducks in a box?

A: A box of quackers.

Earthquake

Q: What do you call a cow caught in an earthquake?

A: A milkshake.

Dog Breed

Q: What do you get when you cross a chili pepper, a shovel and a chihuahua?

A: A hot diggity dog.

Cross a Tiger

Q: What do you get when you cross a tiger with a canary?

A: I don't know. But when it sings, you'd better listen.

Silly
School & Sports

School Silliness

Pirates

Q: Why does it take pirates so long to learn the alphabet?

A: Because they spend years at C.

Glass in Hand

Q: What do you have if you are holding 2 glasses in one hand and 4 glasses in the other?

A: A drinking problem.

Spring Chicken

Q: An older teacher asked her student, "If I say, 'I am a spring chicken,' which tense is that?"

A: Student replies, "It is obviously past."

Student Writing

Teacher: Which hand do you use to write with?

Student: Neither, I always use a pencil.

Music Class

Q: Why was music class so hard?

A: Too many notes.

Always Teaching

Q: Why did the teacher jump in the lake?

A: To test the waters.

---------- ★ ARYA'S FAVORITE

Supply King

Q: Who is the king of all school supplies?

A: The ruler.

Tardy Broom

Q: Why was the broom late for school?

A: It overswept!

Eye Roll

Q: What do you do if the teacher rolls her eyes at you?

A: Pick them up and roll them back.

---------- ★ **ARYA'S FAVORITE**

No Entry

Q: What room can a student never enter?

A: A mushroom.

Ski School

Q: What do skiers like most about school?

A: Snow and tell.

Cross-Eyed

Q: Why was the teacher cross-eyed?

A: She couldn't control her pupils!

Byte

Q: What did the computer do at lunchtime?

A: It had a byte.

Batter Up

Q: Why was the voice teacher so good at baseball?

A: Because she had the perfect pitch.

Switzerland

Teacher: What's the best thing you've learned about Switzerland?

Student: I don't know, but the flag is a big plus.

Sport Silliness

Grasshopper

Q: Why don't grasshoppers watch soccer?

A: They watch cricket instead.

Banking on Football

Q: Why did the football coach go to the bank?

A: To get his quarter back.

Tennis

Q: Why is tennis such a loud sport?

A: The players raise a racket.

Golf

Q: What is a golfer's favorite letter?

A: Tee!

Baseball/Pancake

Q: How is a baseball team similar to a pancake?

A: They both need a good batter.

---------- ★ ARYA'S FAVORITE

Cheerleader Food

Q: What is a cheerleader's favorite food?

A: Cheerios.

Players' Armor

Q: When should football players wear armor?

A: When they play knight games.

Vegetarians

Q: Why don't vegetarians swim in competitions?

A: They hate meets!

---------- ★ **ARYA'S FAVORITE**

Batter Up

Q: Which animal is best at hitting a softball?

A: A bat.

Umpire Weight

Q: Why are some umpires overweight?

A: Because they always clean their plate.

Lazy Exercise

Q: What kind of exercise do lazy people do?

A: Diddly-squats.

Frog Outfielder

Q: Why are frogs good outfielders?

A: They never miss a fly.

Skydiving

Q: What is the hardest part about skydiving?

A: The ground.

Quarterback

Q: What do you get when you cross a quarterback with a carpet?

A: A throw rug.

Astronaut Foot

Q: If an athlete gets athlete's foot, what does an astronaut get?

A: Missile-Toe.

Danger on the Ice

Q: Why can't you tell jokes while ice skating?

A: Because the ice might crack up.

Soccer Ball

Q: Why did the soccer ball quit the team?

A: It was tired of being kicked around.

Catch Me If You Can

Q: What is harder to catch the faster you run?

A: Your breath.

Softball Crime

Q: Why did the policeman go to the softball game?

A: He heard that someone stole second base.

Surfer Trap

Q: Why did the surfer set a trap in the water?

A: To catch a wave!

Basketball Treat

Q: Why do basketball players eat donuts?

A: They love to dunk!

Soccer Success

Q: Why do soccer players do so well in school?

A: They know how to use their heads.

Baseball

Q: What has 18 legs and catches flies?

A: A baseball team.

---------- ★ ARYA'S FAVORITE

Flying High

Q: Why do cheerleaders need a pilot's license?

A: Because they do so many aerials.

Food Fun

Award-Winning Dessert

Q: Who's a dessert's favorite actor?

A: Robert Brownie, Jr.

---------- ★ ALEXA'S FAVORITE

Worst Vegetable

Q: What is the worst vegetable to have on a ship?

A: A leek!

Penguin Pancakes

Q: How does a penguin make pancakes?

A: With its flippers!

Muy Picante

Q: What does a nosy pepper do?

A: Gets jalapeño business!

Comfort Food

Q: Which dessert is perfect for eating in bed?

A: A sheetcake.

He's in the Grave-y

Q: Did you hear about the Italian chef with a terminal illness?

A: He pasta-way.

Blast Off

Q: What's really fast, loud, and tastes good with salsa?

A: A rocket chip!

High Roller

Q: Why couldn't the sesame seed leave the casino?

A: He was on a roll!

Stop Those Cravings

Q: How do most people curb their appetite?

A: At the drive-thru window.

Burned Mouth

Q: Why did the hipster burn his mouth?

A: He drank the coffee before it was cool.

Burning Calories

Person 1: I just burned 2000 calories in 20 minutes.

Person 2: How?!

Person 1: I forgot to take my brownies out of the oven.

Bacon and the Egg

Q: Why did the bacon laugh?

A: Because the egg cracked a yolk.

Vegan Insult

Q: How did Native Americans say vegetarian?

A: "Bad hunter!"

Thankful Milk

Q: What is lactose-free milk's favorite Christmas carol?

A: Soy to the world.

---------- ★ ALEXA'S FAVORITE

Cookie Dentist

Q: Why did the Oreo go to the dentist?

A: Because he lost his filling.

Seating Plan

Q: Why is it annoying to eat next to basketball players?

A: They dribble all the time.

Playground Snack

Q: What candy do you eat on the playground?

A: Recess pieces.

Bread Break

Q: What does bread do on vacation?

A: Loaf around.

---------- ★ ALEXA'S FAVORITE

State Pride

Q: Which U.S. state is famous for its extra-small soft drinks?

A: Mini-soda!

Kids' Drink

Q: What do curious kids drink?

A: HaWHYan Punch.

Airport Chocolate

Q: What kind of chocolate do they sell at the airport?

A: Plane chocolate.

Deviled Eggs

Q: What do you say if you fart after eating deviled eggs?

A: "Eggscuse me."

Straight to the Glutes

Q: Why do hamburgers go to the gym?

A: To get better buns.

Potato

Q: When is an Irish potato not an Irish potato?

A: When it's a French Fry.

Sushi What?

Q: What did sushi A say to sushi B?

A: Wasabi!

Sad Cookie

Q: Why was the cookie sad?

A: Because her mom was a-wafer so long!

Titanic

Q: What was the most popular candy on the Titanic?

A: A lifesaver.

Brain Power

Q: Why did the little boy keep staring at the box of orange juice?

A: Because it said "concentrate."

---------- ★ **ALEXA'S FAVORITE**

The Baker

Q: Why did the baker stop making donuts?

A: She was bored with the hole business.

Cabbage Racing

Q: Why did the cabbage win the race?

A: Because he was ahead!

Hot to Trot

Q: Which condiment has the most kick?

A: Horseradish.

So That's Why They're Red...

Q: Why did the tomato blush?

A: Because it saw the salad dressing.

Celebrations

Halloween

Curvy Spirit

Q: Why do girl ghosts go on diets?

A: So they can keep their ghoulish figures.

Ghostly Roads

Q: What roads do ghosts love most?

A: Dead ends.

House Scream

Q: Why did the haunted house scream?

A: It had window pain.

Maid Service

Q: Why couldn't the skeleton keep anything tidy?

A: Because he has lazy bones.

Ghoulish Soccer

Q: What position do monsters play on soccer teams?

A: Ghoulie.

---------- ★ ARYA'S FAVORITE

Artistic Temperament

Q: Why did the skeleton cancel the gallery showing of his skull-ptures?

A: Because his heart wasn't in it.

Licensed to Fly

Q: What is the favorite mode of travel for skeleton pilots?

A: The scareplane or the skelecopter.

Haunted House

Q: Why are haunted houses like libraries?

A: They have hundreds of horror stories.

Spooky Ghost Parents

Q: What does a ghost call his mom and dad?

A: His transparents.

---------- ★ **ARYA'S FAVORITE**

Witchy Guests

Q: What do witches ask for at hotels?

A: Broom service!

The Guest

Q: Who did the scary ghost invite to his party?

A: Any old friend he could dig up!

Skeleton Music

Q: What is a skeleton's favorite musical instrument?

A: A trombone!

Doing the Dab

Q: What do you call a vampire doing the dab?

A: Count Dabula.

Two Witches

Q: What do you call two witches who live together?

A: Broommates.

Ghost Pilot

Q: Where did the ghost learn to become a pilot?

A: In fright school.

Lonely Hearts

Q: Why did the skeleton cry his eyes out?

A: Because he didn't have any body to love.

Door Not a Door

Q: When is a haunted house door not a door?

A: When it's ajar.

Ghostly Question

Q: Why are ghosts so bad at lying?

A: Because you can see right through them.

Monster Munching

Q: Do monsters eat popcorn with their fingers?

A: No, they eat the fingers separately.

Written in the Stars

Q: How do monsters tell their future?

A: They read their horror-scope.

Vampire Holiday

Q: What would be the national holiday for a nation of vampires?

A: Fangs-giving!

---------- ★ **ARYA'S FAVORITE**

Ghostly Fear

Q: What room do ghosts avoid?

A: The living room.

Inside TV

Q: What kind of TV do you find inside haunted houses?

A: Big-scream TV's.

Thanksgiving

Crazy

Q: Who's the craziest about Thanksgiving?

A: Turkeys. When Thanksgiving approaches, they literally lose their heads!

Colonist Tea

Q: What kind of tea were American colonists searching for?

A: LiberTEA.

Drive-Thru Thanksgiving

Q: What do you call a running turkey?

A: Fast food.

No Church for Turkey

Q: Why can't you take a turkey to church?

A: They use fowl language.

Pilgrim's Ride

Q: What kind of cars would pilgrims drive today?

A: Plymouths.

---------- ★ ARYA'S FAVORITE

Holiday Help

Q: What did the young boy say when his mom wanted him to help fix Thanksgiving dinner?

A: Why me, I didn't break it!

Thanksgiving Relatives

Cannibal One: I just can't stand my mother-in-law.

Cannibal Two: That's quite understandable—why don't you just have the potatoes with the gravy?

Christmas

Addicted to Christmas

Q: How did the ornament get addicted to Christmas?

A: He was hooked on trees his whole life.

Christmas Alphabet

Q: How is the alphabet different on Christmas than any other day?

A: On Christmas, it has Noel.

---------- ★ **ARYA'S FAVORITE**

A Mountain's Favorite Candy

Q: What is a mountain's favorite type of candy?

A: Snow caps.

December

Q: What does December have that other months don't have?

A: The letter D.

Frosty's Cow

Q: What did Frosty call his cow?

A: Eskimoo!

Sad Snowman

Q: How do you know the snowman was sad?

A: 'Cause he had a meltdown.

Pie Eaters

Q: A pie-eating contest was held during the holiday season. What song did they sing?

A: Oh, come all ye facefuls.

That's One Fit Snowman

Q: What do you call a snowman with a six-pack?

A: An abdominal snowman.

Walking Snowman

Q: What do you call a snowman that can walk?

A: Snow-mobile.

Dies in Winter

Q: What lives in the winter, dies in the summer, and grows with its root upward?

A: An icicle.

Reindeer Lessons

Q: Did you hear that Rudolph the Red-Nosed Reindeer never went to school?

A: That's right—he was elf taught.

Failed Snowman Marriage

Q: Why did Frosty ask for a divorce?

A: His wife was a total flake.

- - - - - - - - - - ★ **ARYA'S FAVORITE**

What Do You Call an Old...

Q: What do you call an old snowman?

A: Water!

- -

Snowman Snack

Q: What do snowmen order at fast-food restaurants?

A: An iceberg-er and fries!

Pilgrims

Q: If there were still Pilgrims alive today, what would they be famous for?

A: Their age.

Last
Laughs

Ha! Ha! Ha!

Did You Eat Him?

My 3-year-old brother asked our mom whether I used to be in her stomach.

"Yes," she said.

"How did he get there?" he asked.

"I'll tell you when you're a little older."

"Just tell me this," he said, concerned. "Did you eat him?"

Jack and Jill

Teacher: Jill, where is America on the map?

Jill: Right there, ma'am.

Teacher: Correct. Now, Jack, tell me who found America."

Jack: "Jill.

New Technology

I finally convinced my mother that it was a good idea for her to learn to text. Her first message to me? "Whereisthespacebar?"

Good Genes

The topic for my third-grade class was genetics. Smiling broadly, I pointed to my dimples and asked, "What trait do you think I passed on to my children?" One student called out, "Wrinkles!"

Report Card

Dad: Can I see your report card, son?

Son: I don't have it.

Dad: Why?

Son: I gave it to my friend. He wanted to scare his parents.

Kidnapping

Dad: Did you hear about the kidnapping at school?

Son: No. What happened?

Dad: The teacher woke him up.

Out of It

I overheard one of my cashiers tell a customer, "We haven't had it for a while, and I doubt we'll be getting it soon."

The manager quickly assured the customer that we would have whatever it was she wanted by next week.

After she left, the manager read the cashier the riot act. "Never tell the customer that we're out of anything. Tell them we'll have it next week," I instructed her. "Now, what did she want?"

"Rain."

Stop the Music

"Didn't you used to hear music every time you put on your Western hat?" one cowboy asked another.

"I sure did."

"How did you get it to stop?"

"I removed the hat from my head and took out the band."

First Date

A frog telephones the psychic hotline. His personal psychic advisor tells him, "You are going to meet a beautiful young girl who will want to know everything about you." The frog is thrilled!

"This is great!" the frog said. "Will I meet her at a party?"

"No," says his advisor, "in her biology class."

Stand Up

Teacher: Anyone who thinks he's stupid may stand up! (Nobody stands up at first, then Little Johnny stands up.)

Teacher: Oh Johnny, why do you think you are stupid?

Little Johnny: I don't...I just feel bad that you're standing alone.

Boy, Girl, Boy

Boy: The principal is so dumb!

Girl: Do you know who I am?

Boy: No...

Girl: I am the principal's daughter!

Boy: Do you know who I am?

Girl: No...

Boy: Good! (Walks away.)

Strawberry Cream

A little boy walked into the doctor's office with a strawberry stuck in his ear."Can you help me, doctor?" he pleaded.

The doctor looked closely, and said, "I think I've got some cream for that."

A Fishing Fiasco

My 2-year-old sister went with me to the little trout pond we had in our backyard. I spent a few minutes showing her how to throw the line in the water to catch a fish. Then said, "OK, throw it in." She threw the entire pole into the water.

Also Available from Reader's Digest